Climbing Trees

A Collection of Poems by

Tabitha Jeub

Illustrated by Tabitha & Hannah Jeub

Climbing Trees

First Edition, July 2020
First Printing, July 2020
Copyright © 2020 by Tabitha Jeub

ISBN 978-1-936147-17-5

Monument Publishing
16315 Rickenbacker Ave
Monument, CO 80132
info@MonumentPublishing.com

Printed in the United States of America

Table of Poems

too much to read

books are an illusion of infinity

no one has ever tried to read them all

they've only admitted that that would be impossible

there are shelves, and shelves and shelves

of people discussing theory, philosophy—but mostly themselves

my finger trails across the bounds of books not knowing what i'll find

i want to read them all, but i'm a thousand years behind

i'd be stubborn about it—reading the dumb, the long and the boring

i would read them all—i'd stay up all night

but to my omission there'd be more written in the morning

if only other poets would stop scribbling down what they thought up

if only they'd stop writing so that i could get caught up

caught up on all the new books of phrases being coined

but i guess i'm writing this because

once i couldn't beat them

i joined

absolutes

money doesn't grow on trees

except for dollar bills

man is inherently good

unless he lies or kills

everything is meaningless

except for calculus

you will never learn everything

unless of course you focus

they'll never make a horseless carriage

what about the cars?

if everything under the sun is meaningless

what about the stars?

notice the words you use

be aware of their placements

be especially careful of absolute statements

no matter how beautiful or logical they may be

because there will always be poets to make fun of them

but remember we'll do it eloquently.

a + M = <3

distant music, smoking sticks

you were a drug to me

like a taxed-out toxic

tasteless and thoughtless

taunting me to be less

i treated you like a princess

i've told you that i miss us

you were priceless

but now i'm a prisoner to preciseness

you were my barrier

my cement, my senseless settlement

i didn't mean for this to happen

is it mentally unsettling for me

to recount the sound of lettering?

you were a pretender

pretending to be better than me

our love was like

a disconnected energy

a disaster

a hypocrisy

but i loved you through all of that

loving you was a fact

now i have to subtract

the memories from my brain

to get back on track

with the reality of being sane

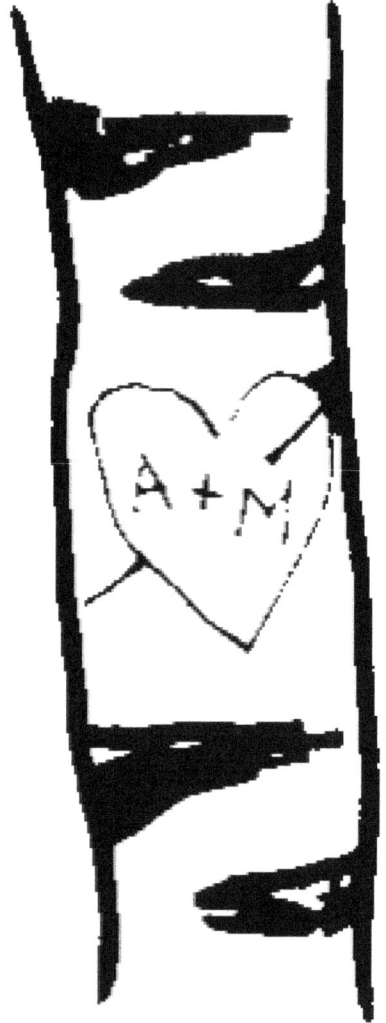

before i write a poem

forces of horses

charge at me

courses of choruses

make me bleed

corpses of choices

are haunting me

taunting me to change

they hate the way

i comprehend

my range of rage

and save scented, mental

sentimental sentences

words descend from the shelf where I sit

they turn into poems and repentances

defended by, spoken by regretful lips

i know it sounds like i'm complaining

but trust me, i'm not

i just think it's nice to write

and no longer be a prisoner of my own thought

befriending the moon

there once was a girl who began her days with a sigh

the hot emptiness of the sun was her happiness' kiss goodbye

at night she would cry, not understanding the darkness

her cheeks would shine in the moonlight, a sad glisten

knowing no one would hold her and no one would listen

alone in this world she laughed with great irony

she didn't speak to anyone of what she felt with agony

one day someone advised her—with a voice that sounded haunted

"even the janitor has something to teach you"

and so she took what she could and left what she wanted

she took every word with a grain of salt

whether it strengthened the message or it was lessened

now, to her every failed friendship was a learned lesson

she befriended the stars and listened to the rain

because its musical beat on the ground made more sense than pain

she spoke with confidence and stood her ground

how great it was to hear the sunshine's sound

and she skipped and danced until the night came to an end

and she was now very grateful to have the moon as a friend

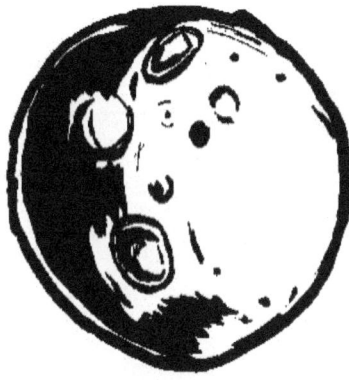

big words come in tiny books

i want to sit

and stiffly sniff

the words of the bible

just for a while

because the textile is so worthwhile

and makes me shyly but slyly smile

the words are perfect, flawless

with my own lists, tricks, and missed underlines

outlining the sinless words

to the blessed verses

i breathe and heath and passionately

feed on the words

i hope the chapters get hung up in my lungs

and the psalms sat and sung

i hope the

words go straight

from my eyes

to the lies in my mind

that way it can be my own little superpower

i'll be good for one more hour

it may seem insignificant to the rest of the world

the highlighted spotted pages that are curled

i have to admit it wasn't me who tore it

but great words come in small books

you only have to be ready to look for it

school

scrunchies and energy drinks

broken backpacks and colored inks

these social norms are trying to catch me

clean soft hair and girl perfume

the tick of a clock in the back of the classroom

i try to pay attention, but the words attack me

chapstick and whiteboards

homework and power cords

i want my daydreams to kidnap me

hoodies and uncomfortable chairs

girls' giggles and boys' stares

i feel this system is trying to trap me.

superficial

compliment me

    please

this contour was no ease

compliment my hair

this was no easy feat

compliment my eyes

and how they're like no one else

but, please don't compliment the things i

    hate about myself

and please don't say anything nice about

    my personality

cause i'll take that stuff seriously

adversely, please don't tell me my

    actions are beautiful

i can't handle that much real

please don't compliment my soul

i can't handle that much feel

just tease me and laugh at the what and the how

    please

can we stick to the superficial for now?

breaking the ice

so, we sat and told stories

awkward at first

but then they flowed like stories should

and i shared things that were weird

and i got over certain things i never thought i would

the words know their power

the words spill across blank pages

filling them with love, hope and rages

the phrases dance and blend

inspiring all who read them

but only the ones who understand

the words of this far-off fictional land

cigarette butts

what will you leave on this earth, friend?

tell me i want to know

he leaves things made out of wood

everywhere he goes

she leaves puzzles all did and done

how many? only god knows

what can you not help but doing, friend?

tell me i want to know

he leaves sketches around his room

some far too worthy to live under his bed

she leaves doodles within the pages of her math book

i wonder how many more are trapped in her head

tell me what you wish to clutter the earth with

please, friend, i want to know

i will leave napkins, receipts and church notes stacked high with my
        poems

how many? i've tried to count, but only God knows

but, please friend, clutter the earth with glory

she deserves that at least

clutter this earth with tasty treats

leave this earth a feast

i beg you, friend, do clutter this earth with wholesome wonders

like gardens, books and rose petals and buds

don't you want to leave more behind than your negative thoughts

and your cigarette butts?

a cloud behind the silver lining

she breathed her last breath
her bones shown through her chest
eating disorders finally killed her, she ran her last lap
but it's fine
at least she had a thigh gap

his head burned; the pain was insane
another pill to accompany his pain
his bank account was too full and he was bored
another glass to swallow the pills he poured
he laid on the floor and stayed on the floor
his landlord wouldn't see his rents
but at least his kids will get a great inheritance

she would never stop drinking
is what he kept thinking
never on time complimented by consistent crimes
she couldn't keep up with the fines no matter what they billed her
good thing too, her addiction killed her

he rolls another dice

he plays another card

the more he plays the worse it gets

fretting, he sets another unsettling settlement

he watches for bluffs he listens for tones

he's addicted, but at least he doesn't have student loans

penny dreams

they say keep your feet on tho ground

and your head out of the clouds

so, i pulled the clouds down

and i danced with them

they told me that dreams turn to dust

so, i dreamt of the stars and sold their star rust

they told me money doesn't grow on trees

but millions of coins and bills are sprinkled in the dirt, the earth and the
    hills

they told me to shoot for the moon and i'll land amongst the stars

so, i shot for the stars and landed in a backward universe

the creatures there told me to breath in the clouds

and keep my feet above the ground

they said to dream of dust and keep my dreams

no matter how dusty

musty

or dirty they may be

they told me to plant my pennies and water them

with liquid copper then

watch them shine and prosper

but they didn't tell me to shoot for the stars

for the stars are not nearly as exciting as watching

dusty dreams glow

penny flowers grow

and to learn everything that the clouds know.

colors rhyme

pink could think with beautiful inky thoughts

like she ought, she fought for her thoughts

she had brink, links and the ability to let them sink in

blue was new, yet had a clue

it could view things as true

it drew—the blue crayon flew

it was valued and beautiful too

but orange was just orange

green was seen as an unforeseen dream

green gleaned

always leaning toward clean jeans and neat things

but orange was just orange

black was in fact flat with a knack

of lacking color in front and in back

never crackling, aching or cracking

just being black and perfect at that

but orange was just orange

every time people went to write or site

a word that rhymes with orange, they failed

orange felt frail and entailed, he would bawl

and bail on the other colors

all because nothing rhymes with orange

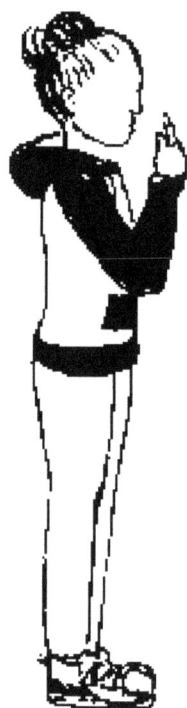
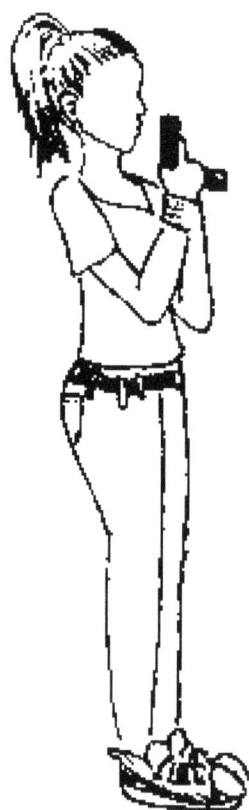

Dying with breath.
Breathing to Live.
Living to death.
Dying to live.

deepness is darkness

gruesome allusion

and gory stories

inspire me

like fear inspires a heartbeat

demon's thrones

i walk through towns of ghosts

i enter demons' thrones

i know that they're alone

and that's how i know i am home

taste of disappointment

i smile brightly then bite my cheeks

i hope i bite

them hard enough

to taste blood

so i can taste blood

instead of disappointment

24

dreaming

one night i fell asleep

a deep sleep, i began to dream

my mind was drifting mindlessly

while my heart was beating noisily

i wanted to live, wanted to be

while my body refused and continued to dream

because my heart was wide awake

as my heart pumped, and flew, i slept, i fell

my soul was awakened then as well

my mind thought i was dying

and then in my dream, i did

i dreamt of meeting celebrities

as my dream turned to lucid

i flew over the hollywood sign

i met walt disney before he died

he even signed my hand, a fine scribble and then a line

the next morning i was tired 'cause my dream had tired me

sleep is supposed to be restful—or so it seemed

but not if your mind always lets you dream

dress to depress

stop depressing yourself

to the point of stressing yourself

and making less of yourself

keep dressing yourself

to impress yourself

put your confidence to the test

and give the whole dress-to-impress thing a rest

because the less you spend making yourself

    look good

the more you will

    look good

natural beauty can only be found in happiness

maybe you haven't tried this, but i would

don't want to write this

the perfect day is where i get everything done that i said i would

the perfect day is being as productive as i could

the perfect day is doing the work that i know i should

if only today were the perfect day

if only my mind would cooperate

if only my mind and heart didn't work alone

if only i'd get to work and stop writing this poem

ego

i think people consider themselves ahead of me

but they need to realize, they need to see

that i have eyes and i can see

that they're judging me

not by who i am

but what i say and what i do

the way i walk

the way i create conversation, talk

they judge based on my actions

and my intentions

so, the tensions of assumption

grow strong in the face of rumors and presumption

but that's okay

assuming you're better than me in every way

is probably

better for me anyway.

expressing expertise

to express exact expertise in essence of experience

you must excel extra excellence of extreme gentleness

exaggerate your kindness

otherwise people will exclude, exchange and excuse

themselves from your presence

press gentleness in all spoken sentences

begin to exist to expand and extend excellence

even and especially in extemporaneous situations.

a stranger named quinn

she existed in this world but didn't act like it

she sounded like an old friend but didn't react like it

she stood like confidence

and sat like oblivion

she smiled like it made sense

and laughed like fairness

everything about her was green

the way she moved

the way her hair was a tease

the way her glasses slid down her nose

her clothes looked the way they're supposed to

she wore her clothes, instead of them wearing her

i wish i'd said "hi" or "hey" or maybe just a glance

but i guess that's just what life is about

ceasing a pointless chance

fake friends

it's precisely preposterous how purposely

dressing pointlessly, perfectly and precious

can potentially participate

in playing a part, a position

in a positively unimportant

process of proposing

a friendship

fifteen

one love

down on one knee

one "yes"

one heart

one wife to be

two years

two kids

two schools

disappointed twice

two more fights

two-faced

"sleep on the couch tonight"

three kids

three jobs

three mommy-what's-wrong's?

trinity

infinity

crying consistently

fourth year, fourth grade

four f's

four start-overs and resets

addiction, contradiction and suspicion

"mom, i'm in love"

four betrayals

false portrayals

four cases of drugs

five broken dishes

five fingers

five men to break wishes

oldest daughter gone

five states away

she says she found the one

no reason to stay

six homes

consistently moving

six thousand dollars in debt

six hopes

being crushed

six new schools to be met

free slushies at 7-eleven

are the only food the kids get

7 days in a week

/ times too weak

several jobs to seek

seven new guys mom brought home

always having to change the number on her phone

seven days of creation

taught in sunday school

but when they got home

mom would tell them jesus was a fool

eight disowned family members

in early september

nine eleven

crushing the twin towers

nine credit cards

taxed out

maxed out

ten digits

ten secrets

ten mistakes

eleven regrets

her son who's eleven

asks a question

"mom, is there a heaven?"

"no honey, just hell"

that stuck with him until he was twelve

twelve bullies

twelve notes in his locker

twelve crude nicknames

and one more mocker

thirteen years old

thirteen cigars

thirteen times he passed out cold

thirteen drugs

too much alcohol

one overdoes

to end it all

2014

all her kids were grown

fourteen lawsuits

fourteen cell phones

fourteen lawyers

all to no use

fourteenth in the courthouse

fourteen years for abuse

her fifteen-year-old son

left on his own

the fifteenth cut upon his arm

fifteen bailouts

fifteen dropouts

fifteen rock bottoms

2015

one pastor

one talk

one to defy any odd

one redemption

one god

one wife, new life

one start again

find yourself in creation

i think going out to venture

finding adventure

in everyday life

everyday texture

is much better

than listening to a lecture

you've got to plug your creativity in and unplug the tension

of this week's lesson

but, let the mountains

maintain, what they were created for

meditation in relation to motivation

use your God-given notation

to take note of creation

it's a blessing

do some testing

on who you really are in motion

fire

burning dangerous intriguing

it wishes to expand, to destroy and leave nothing unharmed

it dreams of warmth and living without alarm

fire wants to burn

wants to strike

it wonders about weather

and greatly fears rain

the thick horrible water and the pain

it likes trees, because they are an easy target

with all those leaves

it believes in freedom

of running wild

it loves open areas

running like a child

it loves brush forests and grass

but also loves to laugh

to smell burnt marshmallows

and young and old fellows

gathered around to talk

and yet

it also plans

to expand

and burn everything in its path

despite its destructive purpose

and the thousands of lost trees

it's a hauntingly beautiful orange glow

that fascinates and terrifies those who see

from right hand to left hand

dear left hand,

i'm doing everything

but you get to wear the ring

and when i get tired, you're

    just not there

i have to brush the teeth,

    lashes and the hair

i can't dance without you

    copying my every

    action

once i move you twitch—a

    reaction

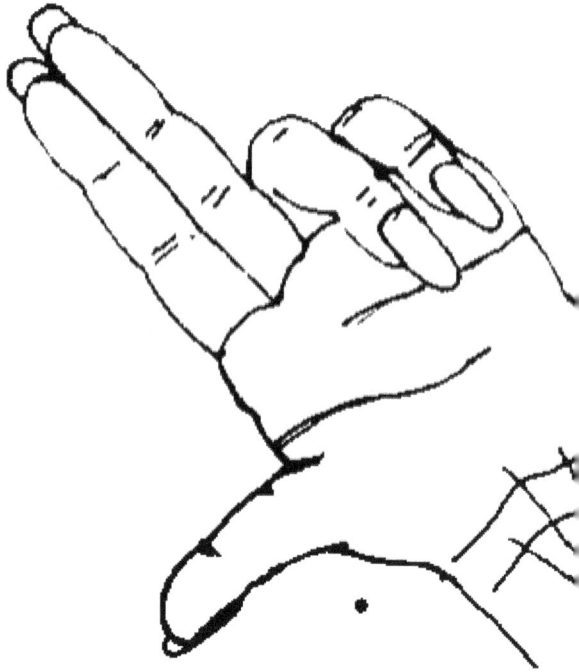

i can paint your nails, but you

    can't paint mine

so i look all sloppy while you

    look perfectly fine

i'm the one doing all the

    cooking, cleaning and

    sweeping

    and you hog the under pillow

when i'm trying to do some sleeping

sorry for complaining

because then again, on the other hand

if it's all synchronized it's much better

i guess it's easier when we work together

i can't write unless you hold the page

and without you there's certain skills i would have never been able to

    master

and with you texting and typing sure does go faster

i don't need you because alone i can snap

but that sound doesn't replace the sound of a clap

and i could play the piano without you,

but it sounds better if you play the other side

and without you my shoes would never be tied

i suppose i better accept that it will be like this forever

i guess some things were just meant to be done together

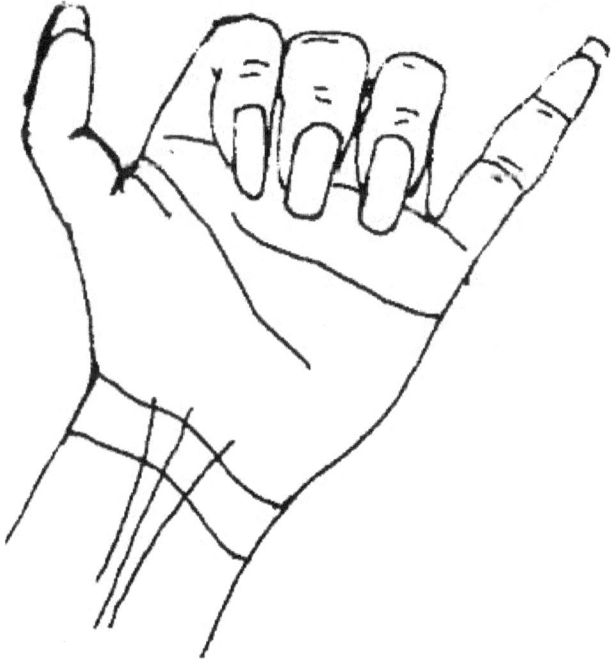

glass girl

glass girl closes her fists

glass girl breaks her wrists

she grips the tub edges and

slips into darkness

glass girl stains herself

her transparent appearance

gives her endurance and deterrence

she'd try to hide her thoughts

but they can see right through her

she'd try to go out in public

but she's scared she'd shatter

she is awake at night

for fear of reflecting the sunlight

God gave us skin so it could be thick

but when you're glass, the words stick.

42

habakkuk now understands *(acrostic)*

absolute beauty comes down

erupting fearfully

God hovered intently

justly

kindly

"look"

men noted onto paper

questions, repentances, sentences

truth unfolded violently

with excellence yet zealousness

and boldness

collided distinctly

evidently from great habakkuk's

    intentions

just keeps loving mindlessly

nothing over priceless quatrains

reading simultaneously together

unbelievably verbal

without excluding

yearning zest

all

because

Christ

does

hating yourself

your mind is loud

your mouth is quiet

life can't be found

you began to hide it

keeping secrets, pointlessly

for no reason, hopelessly

getting out of bed is hard

at night you're scarred

you hate your appearance

people say

"but, you're pretty!"

they're delirious

everyone else seems to like you

sees you like

a confident person

you feel like a weight

a curse on fate

you don't remember the first time

you criticized yourself

you were never bullied

just angry

with your stupid mouth

because you could never decide

which one hurts you more

saying too much

or not enough

heart over mind

love, it's mysterious

parting its way through the fear in us

painting through every particle

peeking through all our personnel

it's personal, but it's practical

parking its data in our hearts

previously leaving with no mark

making the pet peeves

look pretty petty

love, it's curious

preventing the past

hurts from us

consistently containing

the consistency of claiming

persistently reminding

the presence of personality

it's best if (seemingly worse if) love calls for service

but love calls for the necessity of vulnerability.

without it, relationships are just surface

hitler

salt, pepper and sugar

were all good friends

they lived in a town

just around the bend

one sunny day

ginger came to say

that sugar was the best of all

so he killed all the pepper

in slow decay

he captured all the sugar

in spicy dismay

and locked the salt

sweetly away

coach

he told a moral

with a story at the end

once upon a the end

he took the author from the quote

he spoke exactly what he wrote

he asked a question to answer the question

he began with a conclusion

and finished with his introduction

he explained a reality

to understand a metaphor

he wasn't nice

but he was okay

because he used the words like he used money

unsparingly, wisely and in just the right way

part i: poetic words & where to find them

a tree grows in brooklyn

a beautiful sight to see

everyone who saw this tree

was quick to take note and notice

the oak

whose branches were soaked with ink

and cloaked in poetic sounds

its roots were made of purpose

purposely rooted in prosperous ground

surrounded by earth made of dirt and words

its center was hidden

hollow and forbidden

ridden of anything sinful and dull

the tree that grew in brooklyn

was full of branches, lashing and catching birds

whose names were symbolic of words

the robins lived in the highest of branches

the branches made up of sentences

the jays lay in the lower branches among the leaves

leaving behind streams of dreams

the birds and insects that lived in the tree that grows in brooklyn

collected selected poetic sounds

syllables, conjunction and punctuation

and made their nests of the rest left over

commas and exclamations

the leaves of the tree grew far and stretched over the words

the leaves were letters, the alphabet

bent and sent into absence

48

the birds were known to eat the letters

the cluttered importance of poetic mutters and mumbles

p's were probably the most popular

particularly, perfect and precisely precious

the p's were found among the leaves

pressed with practiced potential into the tree

r's were radically rare

they were always where

the rotten ration of leaves were

they raced to the ground

where they were raked up

and never found

but, the most interesting thing about this tree that grew in brooklyn

was the way people looked at it

and looked for it

poets would gather their feathers and letters

pack up their pens and paper

and seek the tree whose leaves were needs

poets and writers would trim and clip and take the bark

and start work of art

they took the words and put them to use

they called them poems, music and news

they used the words for things they called books

they'd look at the brooklyn tree

and build fences made of sentences

of course, the tree was not defenseless

keeping the best and priceless words

to itself

undiscovered, beautiful wording

hidden from the world

the tree was never offended

nor defensive

it was honored that the humans

loved its bent bunched branches

the tree understood

that its roots and wood

inspired others

and inspiration is very different from imitation

imitation has a limitation

whereas inspiration is endless

and that's the whole story

the core and origin of words

woods and birds

inspiration can be found, friend

just depends on where you are lookin'

i recommend starting with the tree that grows in brooklyn

hold your tongue

funny how doing nothing can be so complicated

calculating an opponent's next move can't be more anticipated

waiting hurts more than fighting

letting time pass hurts more than battle scars

unpredictability is more paralyzing than action

when evil is around the corner

when your breath is louder than your heart

when every inch of you is surrounded

by the loudness of the dark

stopping a clock takes more focus than breaking it

silence proves a point more than debating it

in a world where everyone wants to be noticed

shouting, yelling, and protesting

being quiet is a good way not to be missed

'cause this world has a shortage of listeners

when every word, insult and counter argument

are fighting at your lips like jail broken prisoners

being strong is being quiet

holding still, holding your breath

takes more energy than running

even from the pits of your own death

years spent on barriers, barricades and foundation

are not nearly as exciting as war

but just as necessary

when standing up for what you live for

the gravest mistake a man can make

is acting before even thinking to think

and the strongest thing a man can do

is to be first to turn his own cheek

how i will leave this world

people who think too much about their life, i call them fools

my teacher told me to begin with the end and end with the beginning

but i've never been one to follow the rules

i was born into this world crying, with my hair bouncing and curled

so, i'll leave this place smiling, my head more on straight than this world

how is one to succeed?

who?

when?

what?

why?

where?

how?

who must i ask? the wise, the experienced who have been?

and i'm still so young

If I am supposed to start, when?

what states, what major, what purpose is there?

and beyond all that, i must ask, where?

why am i supposed to succeed now?

and my final question is, of course, how?

guilty

somedays i lay

awake and shake

afraid to say—

just to admit

to my brain,

that i have not

refrained from sin

i've framed

my sin and claimed it

i base my life on hiding it

i take the guilt and shame

and fear its flame

i cram my shame into a can

until i can believe it's not real

instead of dealing with

how real it is.

i peel back grass

fast and

fasten a shovel

in my hands.

i shove it in the gravel

it travels and unravels an unholy whole hole

i shove my crammed shame

in the hole

and bury it

quick enough

just so i can sin again

which i always tend to do

      again

and again

and again

if

i hate this process of deciding whether or not to grow up

this practice of debating whether or not to give up

if i do grow up, i lose the best gift—my childhood

if i don't, i lose an eternity of innocent good

the reality is that either way i would

i would lose that should have

i could lose that want-to

that ambition, that could-have

if i were only brave enough, if i only knew

if i could only know the how

if i could have years of experience, right now

i hate this process of asking "how" and the task of "if"

because nothing will prosper if i ask "if"

i suspect the fake respect of people

because they're proud if i'm caught up

which made me neglect certain subjects

when they were brought up

i purposely sought and thought of

anything but sex, alcohol and

    beer

because i was brought up and

    taught to fear

to listen and to hear

that imagination didn't matter

    compared to a career

they taught me to outline my

    passions

to pretend i care

'cause pretending was better

    than nothing

to fake optimism for the

    opportunity

honestly for the ingenuity

genuinely, sharing my thoughts generously

but only the thoughts people wanted to hear

only adults, my "elders"

don't share the thoughts that would interest my peers

they told me to be myself

but didn't understand my humor

they taught me to see myself

as nothing but a failure

unless i fulfilled someone else's dream

part ii: the day i met the words

quotations are endlessly in rotation in my head

many people want to write

in my sight, i *need* to write

i might need a keyboard in the light

and slightly crave a pen at night

i need paper in the mornings

people worry and think that i'm mourning

scorning me for all the adoring words i do

of course, i ignore the warnings and warm up to a

pencil and pen

often, i send the wrong message

to people who aren't one with the pen

they don't understand

the fictional land

filled with people who catapult their words into the world

this world is filled with people

who turn their chitter-chatter into titter-tatter

if you could hear the typewriter clicking away through my thoughts

i thought if i fought the noise that annoys me

and sits itself on a dark shelf in an empty room in my head

never to be seen, never to be found

but the more i fight the dreading, dead sound

i find i am bound to the pound of the keys

i was crowned the queen of the words

my thoughts handed me the keys to poetry and my imagination led me to

   a dormitory

where they discussed glory and worry

and other words that sounded poetic

sympathetically my psyche
who wore lipstick and limped
        quickly on a walking
        stick
handed me the rich trick to
        arithmetic
and taught me how to rhyme
people say it's a crime to be
        alone all the time
it's no crime to lay in bed
        and play with
        sentences in my head
but honestly i'd rather that
        than be keen to being
        seen
besides, that's what it
        means to be crowned
        queen

if the moon died

you look at life like a periodic table

all colors, all numbers, patterns to words

there's no patterns to people

no cookie cutter quiz

and yet you trust the sun to rise

you put your faith in the way the weather comes

but you can never really be sure

the moon could die

and have a wonderful funeral

i bet the stars would sing

the sun would preach

the earth would cry

maybe saturn would wipe earth's tears

and mars would read from the bible

i like things that most people hate

i like things that most people hate

like being stressed out when things aren't going my way

it reminds me to remind me that everything's okay

it allows me to remind me that someone bigger is in control

and it's ok to not know

what or where to go

being a little stressed

a little tested

and fed up in a mess is good for my ego

it reminds me that i'm not all that

i'm not the bee's knees

in fact, it's the littlest of worries that makes life worth living

that makes us, every day, thankful to breathe

i like things that most people hate

like when it starts pouring and you've got a long ride home

so, you fall like the rain, to sleep like you ought

it's not negative, nor positive, but it's what you've got

when the sun is setting and you're driving down a lot

the sun dashes from in and out of the trees

trying to decide if it should blind you or not

or when you don't have a car or a ride

so, you're forced to sit and think of something to think of in your head

no entertainment, so you watch the world move around you instead

being sore in the morning after a long yesterday

because it reminds you that you worked hard in its own way

i love things that most people hate

eating too much and laying down in pain

cause that one extra muffin was worth the ache

falling down when trying to ice skate

because your cuts and

    scrapes remind you

    that you attempted

    something great

getting turned down for a

    second date

that's okay i wanted to be

    alone anyway

when things take too long

so you appreciate the wait

and let your patience

    expand

it reminds you that you had

    good parents

and a short life span

when you're not sure when

    someone's joking, so

    instead of laughing

    you stall

and when you do laugh you

    laugh too loud or

    forget to laugh at all

when the sarcasm gets too

    real

that no one knows you're joking, and you look like a jerk

and too many layers of jokes stack up like homework

the right person will chuckle at your humor

then you know for sure that you can care for her

i like things most people would call ugly

cause glasses and braces give a blank face character

bad movies and crappy coffee leave a wide-open area for common
     ground

'cause shared interest over ugly colors is as fun as digging through a
     lost & found

when a stranger and you at the same time say "hello"

and then, "have a great day"

then "you too" you both say

then awkwardly wave

attempting to wave the moment away

trying to save your first impression in some way

or when friends cancel plans, so you have to stay home all day

which at first is dismay, but you decide it's okay

because you find things to do

like test your coffee making skills

literally starting from the ground up

stretching from lattes, to mess ups, to mochas

then stretching and trying out yoga

i think it's fun to be sick

once you overlook it

you'll be sweaty, ill and fretting

but you will be alone, and so you listen to yourself breathe

and you watch yourself dream

not a lot to be said

just you, your computer and your bed

when a distant relative writes you a note

when you thought they didn't care

and maybe they don't but you put the note in a box and keep it there

66

i like dirty things that most people hate

when a car seats six people and you've got eight

when books get dusty on top

so you cough and sloppily wipe them off

i marvel in the simplest of mistakes

a silly accident is all it takes

when rain makes bible pages wetter

cause children's scribbles and coffee stains makes a good book better

when crumbs are scattered across the carpet floor

'cause that way it's more satisfying to vacuum

the perfect chore

there's just something about the smell of burnt marshmallows, rubber
      and the fruit in a local store, that leaves you wanting more of those
      simple mistakes than before

i like things that most people hate

and i like to think that that's okay

if you focus on things you love and the things you know

it's hard to be mad at the things that are out of your control.

imitating me

i wish i were nice to people,

and ladylike

a smiling, nice girl that everyone liked

saying everything right

i wish i wasn't mean

bombastic and overly dramatic

accidentally being sarcastic

instead of saying what i mean

and maybe playing high status

i wish i could fake a smile

instead of savoring a real one for a while

i'm out of practice, see?

i guess i'm just bad at imitating me

being human

stumbling, fumbling shows weakness,

but, being humble shows strength

longevity of vocabulary does not prove intelligence

but, the width of one's wit also proves length

the ability to fearlessly show vulnerability

doesn't mean you're emotional

the capability to prove your feeling's capacity

only shows you're human and you're rational

jack-in-the-box

wind me up

make me jump

i am so sorry i scare you

when you force me to pop up

sing me your song

your rhymes and remarks

shut me in my box

and leave me in the dark

i guess it's easier to think of you in here

than face your commands

it's easier to think of me in here

than face your demands

just as it is easier to pretend than to face our fear

of where this all ends

72

alone

"i know everything," said the man

said the woman, "i've learned all i can"

they apparently knew everything there was to know

they'd seen all there was to be shown

and then they eloped and then they died alone

parents

other kids don't get to see their parents kiss each other

other kids don't get to see their parents miss each other

and list each other as each other's best friends

it tends to be dysfunctionality is the trend

some kids grow up with their parents screaming at one another

i don't think they really knew if their father loved their mother

my father would wear an apron

making pancakes with maple

completely incapable and unable

to keep his eyes off his wife

this is rare

other kids get three or four moms in their life

it is kind of gross, two adults unbelievably head over heels

they almost never argue, it sounds more like making deals

even though it does get ridiculously boring

they jump to tell their love story like little kids jump to listen to a bedtime
    story

and they tell it like the first time, like we haven't yet discussed it

i know my mom loves my dad

and so i will not complain because i am so privileged to be disgusted

i write to stay sane

god gave me my poems

he sprinkles them into my brain

and i thank him for that

because they keep me sane

judge a book by its cover

people can talk and make others impressed

but people would listen if they focused on how they were dressed

functionality should never be sacrificed for aesthetics

they say "beauty" shouldn't be skin deep

but to ignore first impressions and appearance

is quite the logical leap

one could have a gift for persuading and be a master of debate

but the audience would pay attention if they stood up straight

one could be the smartest in the room

never missing or lacking a fact

but it means nothing without posture and eye contact

a product could be studied with credibility

tested initially to test the ability

created with the utmost functionality

it could be put to the test and let others

pry it and try it

but listen, if it doesn't look good, no one will buy it

i understand all of this is outside appearance and looks

but a creative title and cover is the success for best-selling books

master of language

allow me to introduce to you a man i once met

a man who kept different sentences as pets

he could carry the best stories in his pockets

and pass them out when necessary

he would unwrap passion delicately

and unleash it appropriately

he would take his words

and recognize them, he would line them up and organize them

he spoke as if passion was having a chat with him

the metaphors obeyed his every action

the haunting, purposeful pauses swayed with him

he danced with the words

his voice kissed the children's ears

they listened silently

his hand motions were always a pleasant surprise

and the morals of his thoughts burned through his eyes

like his eye contact contained a certain way of being entertained

so if you do get to meet this master of language

i would say have a chat, smile, and learn what you can

　　but instead i'll say be careful—he can persuade anyone and any man

a mindful thought for a thoughtful mind

collections of memories

cluttering parts of me

making the best of me

and taking the rest of me

boxes of thoughts

rotting in the slots

amongst lots of other caught thoughts

killing my memories

filling the rest of me

shelves of alphabetized realizations

organized, civilized nations

fathoming the worst of me

gathering the rest of me

totes of guilt,

sit and wilt,

covered up and smothered under filth.

murdering the thoughts underneath

and furthering the rest of me

framed images

stacked and hung

the do, the did, the done

mixing my memories

fixing the rest of me

the past

holding onto the old

will slowly mold you into fool's gold

warm hands, cold heart

tearing you apart

starting from the inside and working its way out

targeting your insecurities

pretending they're realities

forming your fears

warding them out in the form of tears

this thing will tell you there's no cure

for what you hear and hold dear

these lies, they'll peel at the surface as you peer

beat the statistic

by remembering your past and remembering not to keep it

let go of your past, and of last month's misery

focus on the present because it's a gift

and yesterday is history

my hands don't get paid

my thumbs have learned to keep what they earn

by quickly and sternly typing poems, phrases and expressions

excess words and unwired thoughts without internet access

my fingers are long and boney

people ask if i play piano

no, i say, my fingers are trained

to stay straight late into the night

lightly typing fiction and written light

my fists are clenched and cold

they know that the pen will find them

fold them and make them hold onto old, holes in pages

and the whole of stages in writing

my hands are skilled

willed and built to tilt words into verses and poetry

clauses and purposeful pauses

all from two hands

a few strands of paper

eight fingers that stand

racing across screens

and spacing, unseen

my mind, my hands, the ink

let it sink in

my mind strives for perfection

my hands stick to what they know

showing no weakness

as if my subconscious doesn't know

that they mess up and miss up

slip up, screw up, miss spell

82

and fail to tell the whole story

because it's all to my mind's glory

it might be because of my heart's might

and that my hands flight is not right

they can't coexist

they keep me up at night

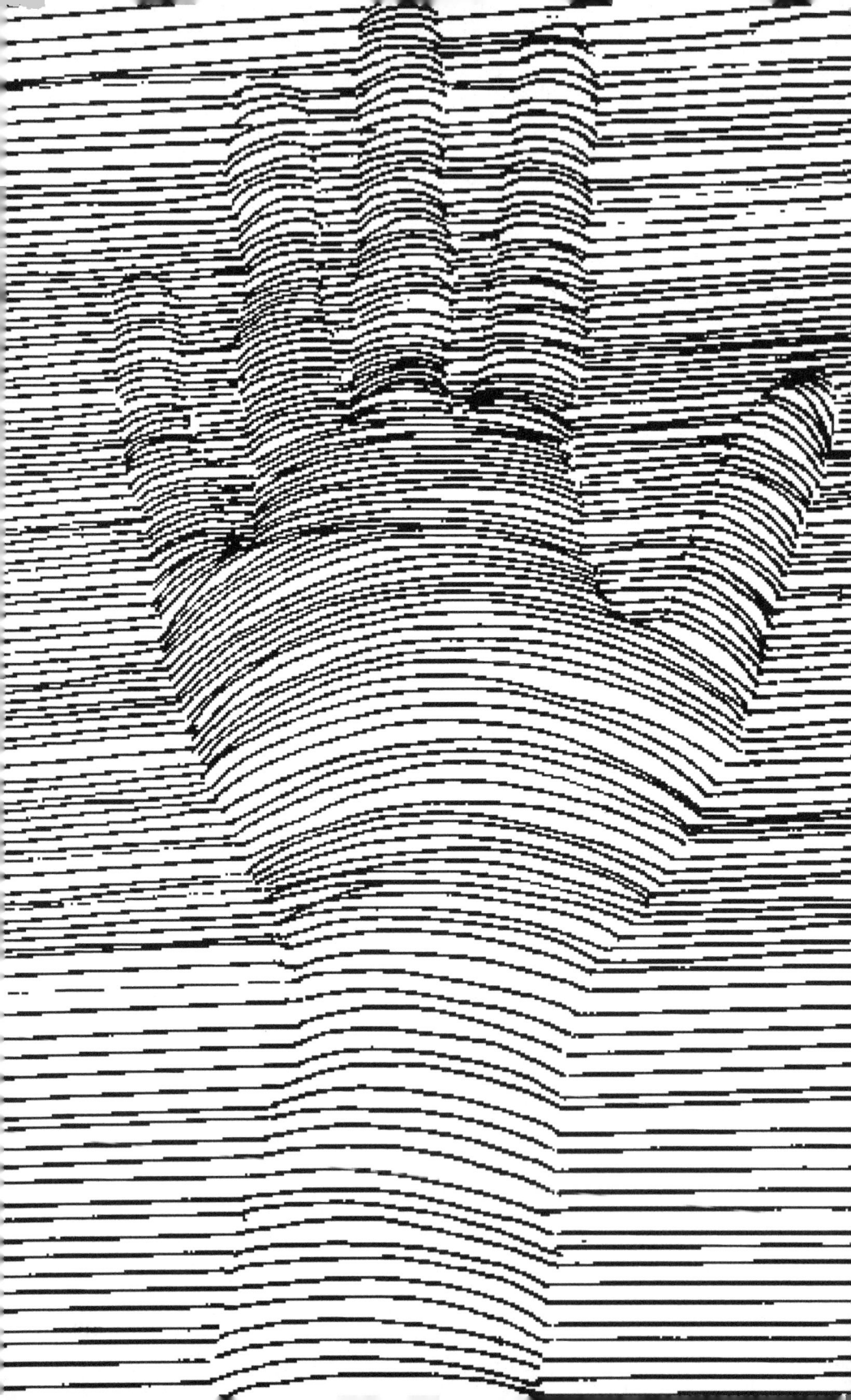

my opinions are best

look at my opinions

aren't they nice and shiny?

just look at my opinions

the large, round, colored and

     tiny

this one is unfolded

surrounded by my worldview

and something that i think i

     heard when i was about

     two

this one is my favorite

because it never changes

no matter what facts have

     been stated

or what stages the statistics

     are cited from which

     pages

this one i don't understand

but isn't it grand?

that i can entertain a thought without accepting it?

this one is dark and buried

i haven't been able to properly dig it up and reap it

but i've never bothered to try, so i keep it

just look at my opinions

aren't they nice and strong?

this opinion is shallow

even i try to hide in my shadow

it's not that i am ashamed or anything

it's just that i think that you think that i think

that i would be ashamed of me

this one is small

but it's the heaviest

something that seems obvious

but also the one i know the most about

if only i had the courage to sprinkle it around

this opinion used to be solid

i'd call it grounded and founded upon steady ground

and pounded into the proudest parts of my brain

but all it took was a fact or two

and a moment of nothing short of fury

for it to be melted and liquidated

back into nothing but a theory

sometimes my opinion of people

turn from innocent

to black

because i judge their actions, not their intentions

and their rumored ones at that

oh, look at this opinion

it is the biggest one i own

it fits only outside

and it always sits alone

on the surface it is irrational, and controversial at least

but just inside and just underneath

are countless hours of research, skepticism and disbelief

evidence for both sides and a conclusion of relief

so welcome to this canal of words

and opinions that to me are normal

and i hope to you are absurd

i made up my mind

put them into my mind and called them my own

i'll admit my opinions don't give proper credit

not transcript—ed, but more manipulated

most of my opinions were stolen

taking bits and pieces of other written theses

and even sometimes the whole

and then rewritten

from a book i never finished

and one line from a radio show

i took two opinions and i decided to believe them

in fact, it's just like that

i balance most of them right between

belief and fact

would you like to take a look at my opinions?

or maybe buy a few?

i'll pass them out and make a profit

maybe i'll make a fortune off it

say, where are you going?

don't you want to hear all my opinions?

and all the things i have decided on knowing?

hey, come back— you

before my opinion of you turns black too

night owl or early bird?

are you a night owl or an early bird?

do you prefer colorful leaves or instead the silhouette of trees?

do you love the sound of wolves and crickets at night?

or rather the sound of birds saying good morning to the sunlight?

do you rather the morning air bite you on your nose and ears?

or the dark of the night biting on your fingertips and fears?

do you love purple mountains, or do you like green ones?

and do you think the millions of stars are better than just one sun?

do you like the coldness of sunrise?

and don't you love to see your breath to remind yourself that you're
      alive?

do you like the stars closing for the moon, or the stars being the sun's
      grand reopening?

and is going to bed early worth missing the sunset?

or is it worth the amount of sleep that you're going to get?

and how many nights do you have to stay out late

to begin to miss the sunrise?

or is your excuse that you cannot get out of bed even on the 10th or the
      11th of tries?

there's no right answer to these questions

but keep these handfuls of thoughts in the back of your head and ask
      them of yourself over and over again

and— what? who, me? well thanks for asking, friend

i am everything in between

maybe a night bird or an early owl

i want everything there is to be seen

if the sun rose at 3 a.m. i'd be up—you know i would

if only the night were forever

i'd never sleep—if only i could

and i've stayed up to greet the stars because i missed you

and to go on an adventure i'd be up before the sun if i could be with you

because there's something irresistible about the morning's haunting
   stillness

even if it's warm or it's a morning of the chilliest

and there's something about the excitement in the night

something about mystery, or just being out of sight

i mean can't you imagine an old owl waking up to see the morning and
   then napping later in the day?

and can't you see a little bird staying up past the moon just to play?

sometimes all this can be inconvenient and sometimes we collide

but i have to say maybe all night owls have a little early bird inside

nap

i want to take a nap

to pull the words over me and push the words out from under my pillow

i want the little words to snuggle up close to me, so i can sleep warmly

maybe i could have tea, the cinnamon kind, the one that makes me write

i want to sleep and dream of flying, i want to never look at phone

    screens again

i want to sleep and never talk to anyone again

the sheer elegance of sleeping with nothing but the comfort of the words

    sounds more delightful than going on the town, going shopping or

    dining in

but of course, i must write something because apparently, i can't keep

    still unless a certain rhyme, thought or story shines in

october skies

october is

that awesome time of year

where dark winter clouds

flirt with summer stars

opportunity

opportunity

it's an absurd word

often misused and misheard

what i feel is—um

it's always said out of fear

or optimism

i tend to notice the fear

or pretend i didn't hear

opportunity isn't always

an option of career

you won't be any nearer to failure

if you opt out of an optimistic opportunity

not every event is sent by the big guy

some things are simply meant to pass by

here's a seemingly seemed metaphor

that seemed to sew itself into the core

when learning to simply speak

about specific speech

to publicly speak and not be afraid

you're taught to think, speak and

persuade

with opportunity you should simply

think, speak and pray

that way optimism is sure to stay

paper boy

your pencil opinions

are sketched in my heart

your inky lies sink into my eyes

when i try to sleep at night

i hear your scissor words

cutting my ears

bringing me to tears

you cut out the bad in you

and glue it to me

you tape your insecurities

to my already shaking knees

your hands are chalk,

they shed powder when you walk

they'll outline my body

once you've killed me with your talk

your eyes are magnifying glasses

all you ever ask is

where my mask is

you hate the reality

of when our lips meet

'cause all you ever see is the ugly in me

your face is cardboard

a mask you made yourself

of course you can't afford

smooth, fake stealth

your skin is paint

leaving faint, physical traits

everywhere you touch and everywhere you go

dark colors slipping and dripping down to your toes

your mouth is an eraser

i'm scared you'll erase me

just like you erased her

you speak lies of cover ups

mopping up and soaking up

your dark past

one day you'll choke it up

and everything will crash

the colors on your skin will clash

and even the smallest lies will last

forever pasted onto your painted skin

the lies will consume you

until you can't breathe

you'll heave and then you'll leave me

and scream that you need me

but at last the lies from your past

will smother you until

it appears to be an accidental kill

but, if you die, i'll be painted blue

i admit i loved you—thus, i'll die too

pencil

i *wood* love to use a pencil

if it weren't for its enchantment

and my attachment to that

    wonderful smell

of school days and art

a smell of greying papers under a

    lead dart

an orange peel of plastic

strong, significant and enthusiastic

a magic wand, fond of a skillful hand

willing to create

spilling and overfilling with chills

and dark gray representations of love and hate

the shiver–erupting scribble

like a song—or a chime

used for the best of times

the brilliance of math, the numbers smudged and then collapsed

from the long duration of equation

and a math–major, a pencil in hand, with caution and persuasion

or used for the writers

needing a battle weapon

sharp enough to etch their descriptions

their emotions and projections

used for the worst of times

etching out poems, and coping with the ups, downs and alones

wishing that this wood–coated bullet

will get them through the life outside of math and art

a shot in the dark

a hope of making the line, reaching the mark

used for drawing out crowds of people

to see a peephole, a neat group of souls

that don't exist outside of paper

almost hoping they were real, ignoring the deception

and staring at the false reflections in the artist's creation

and the lead people will stare back

their hearts heavy

their eyes beady

their tin bodies beg for oil

but the sketcher locks them within the pages of their books

a double lock, impossible to escape

so, there they stay, maintaining perfect shape

one day they'll be set free

maybe a hundred, maybe thousands, maybe just three

sometimes it makes more sense that people were drawn

their souls etched and sketched with several strokes

maybe thought up on a napkin, on paper or on cardboard

just think how many people's souls have been pencil poked

provoked by a small instrument more dangerous than the sword

play dumb and learn

a second guess and double check is the greatest habit of all

thinking that one is always right is man's greatest fall

asking a good question is a skill rarely practiced

a sharp mind equals an opportunity scarcely missed

humility is a sign of relevance

saying "i don't know" is a sign of intelligence

looking dumb for the sake of learning

is the mark of a highly educated mind

if you fake it all the time

you're guaranteed to fall behind

i say this to you

but you can do what you do

just know that once these words leave my mouth

i will turn right around and read this poem to myself

poet's pen

my master uses me when she's inspired

she uses me when she's upset

she scribbles delicately

because her thoughts are in debt

she has schedules to be met

and more to set

because her thoughts don't stop

she's constantly inspired

an electric clock

while she sleeps, i'm on watch

i watch for flocks of thoughts

and herds of memories

for whispers of tendencies

i try to work with her mind

i've tried to be kind

i've tried to find some common ground

but it seems she can't remember anything

unless i write it down

possessions

materials materials

possessions possessions

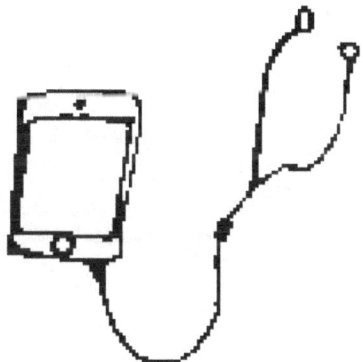

i would help you, but i must

    post a picture of myself

i would talk to you but i'm

    texting someone else

materials materials

possessions possessions

i would travel the world, but never without my phone

and i would go out with you, but this makeup doesn't match my tone

materials materials

possessions possessions

i'd rather text you than say it to

    your face

cause it's less pressure to click

    send or click space

yes, let us have a conversation

let us discuss the when, the why

    and of course the how

but, shh shh! before we do, i must tell the world that i'm eating right now

materials materials

possessions possessions

call me ugly, annoying, obsessive and the next

but don't you dare not accept my friend request

yes, do lay down and have a rest

but please, please don't ignore my texts

materials materials

possessions possessions

life is all about the filter, the better the stricter

as long as i look nice in my profile picture

let's not talk to each other anymore

let's skip the love and obsession

let's go back to silence

and the materials materials

and the possessions possessions

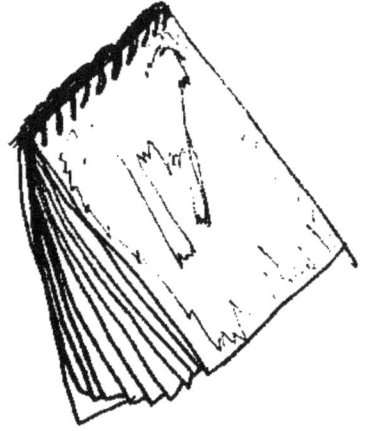

reading the bible

i underline the lines that make sense to me

i skip over sentences that bother me

i smile at things i already know

i avoid the void of thing i hadn't known

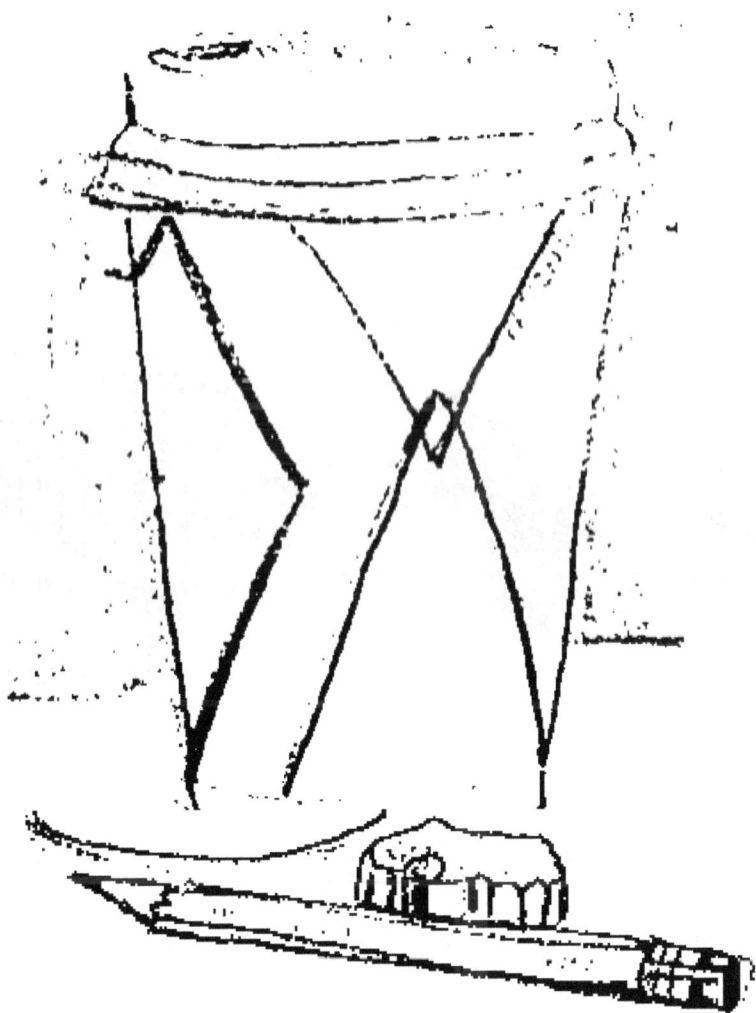

realize

he has real eyes

a nice smile

i think it's time i realize

he only knows me by profile

things can be lies and things can be real

but i have to realize

that there can be real lies

reasons to smile

often times i get down and i forget to smile

but there's a few things that make me happy

if only for a while

like the way my beautiful sister talks in her sleep

or my little sister's macaroni and cheese

mother's long, beautiful nails

little brothers' bragging about how he turned four

when my sand-colored dog dreams, she moves her tail

how my writer friends remind me that i've told this story before

my beautiful sister's high-pitched laugh

lipstick stains on my mom's wine glass

multicolored skinny jeans

converses with leggings

big sweaters over boy shorts

a middle school friend's tennis court

large cups of iced tea and coffee flavored candy

the part where annie names the dog sandy

beating my older brothers at anything

big backyards and tire swings

when mother laughs under her breath

how my beautiful sister loses it when she's stressed

when big brother claims that he's the best

waking up to a conversation

when little kids first hear the story of creation

how my old friend laughs at nothing

how a recent bride smiles consistently

when old friends say hi

when pastors make the entire audience cry

how little sister's pants are always jeans

eating outside, hotdogs and beans

our outdoor campfire

father naming things "adventures"

sleeping in hotel beds or getting a new sled

hauntingly beautiful voices of girls

the way mother wears her pearls

and my beautiful sister's attempts to wear pigtails

when one of your best friends gets a haircut

when an elderly person says the word "butt"

all in all, count your blessings

smile at the little things

write all day

if i could stay home and write poems all day

trust me i'd want to

but i wouldn't

you need to have those moments where you finally do something that
      you

thought you couldn't

you need to feel stressed

in order to feel relaxed

sometimes you need to not know what will happen next

in order to know what skills you lack

you will never grow if you're always comfortable

you will never live if you only do the things affordable

comfort zones are the thief of adventure

to venture outside of this zone is where growth is centered

i could write poems endlessly, trust me

but if i wasn't living fully and figuring life out

what in the world would i write about?

ribcage

my ribcage

is supposed to cage my heart

so that it doesn't hurt so bad

like a maze inside a cave

where no one can go

but my heart will try to beat

and defeat my ribs

and find a way out of its cage

unfortunately, my rib cage is weak

somehow the feelings

get to me

roger owens

he called me interesting

before i had a chance to tell him about school, work and family

he called me beautiful

before i had a chance to do my hair and put on a dress

we talked of life

places and this world's lack of common sense

and he called me fascinating

because we spoke of ideas instead of events

scars

i've got scars on my face

from stress

stressing and being depressed

stressed to impress

stressed out from trying to stress less

what to wear—how to dress

stressing from not confessing my

infestation of sins

i've got a thin scar on my chin

from sledding and embedding and letting my body

caress down pact snow

i have to stress the fact, though

that i was trying to impress

and slipped down the cliff of death

i've got backne, scars from acne

covering my neck down, from my chest

around, to my back

also, from stress attacks

i've got a scar on my lower back

from lack of safety in our backyard

scared from a large chunk of metal

that fell too far and settled

into my skin,

skinning and pinning me down

no blood, so i've got a brown

crown shaped scar from that metal bar

i've got a scar on my arm

from construction in our yard

i slipped on the gravel,

making me travel, slipping

on the landscaping

scraping my arm in alarm

on a jagged nail

i've got scars around my fingernails

from hangnails

and skin that's failed

to stay entailed to my fingertips

of course, i don't help by itching

and stitching and picking a

    biting

the fighting skin

i've tried rinsing and rubbing lotion

but no matter how hard i try

my skin stays dry

some of these scars are dumb

like the scar beneath my thumb

that i've only come to tell a few people

cause i feel uncomfortable

let's move on now before i cry

or worse—lie

let's move to my thigh

a trampoline spring

bouncing, then falling and landing

and cutting my leg exceeding my worries

bleeding through my jeans

where that spring cut clean

now i've got a lightning looking scar

from a trampoline bar

i've got cuts on my knees

from things i don't remember

probably in september

climbing pines and embers

from ice water, in the ice–cold winter

the days got warmer

my shorts got shorter

my legs got tanner

and my knees got beaten, skinned clean

from trees and unseen splintering

my knees, like anybody's

were abused

accurately accused of

misused tissue

i've got scars on my shins from clumsiness

and accidents

from trampolines and other dents

and lastly, my feet and toes

my big toe is smashed and crushed

from that ratchet bent unbalanced bench

that tipped and nipped my toe

to which i tripped

my toe bled and led to a series

of long-lasting baths

a ton of medicine

i tell you all this

because my body's been bent

and bruised and spent

but now i have scars

my own little memories

telling childhood stories

of games and of glory

neat little marks

book marking and highlighting

the darkest and most exciting

parts of my story

fighting to be remembered

terrified to forget

dying to be heard

bearing embers of words

stitched on the surface of my skin

all the stories let out

forced to be asked about

and talked about

discussing disgusting tales

of all the fails and miss rails

and untraveled trails

that your body put there for you

natural tattoos

i want you to know

that it's drastically untrue

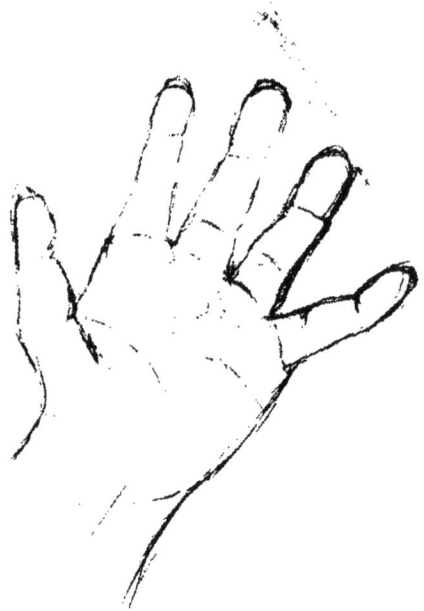

those are beautiful

eventful, purposeful

moments and events

secrets forever etched

each scar is a mark, a tick

a terrific tick mark

showing what you did and what you do

specific and unique

to you and only you

small talk

cool glasses

but i really don't care about your sight

i am glad you're here, friend

let's not talk about your flight

yes, we can talk because now we are together

please, let's skip what day it is and discussing the weather

i'd rather know what deep thoughts you've had

than know how much you earned

i don't care of the places you've been

tell me what you learned

i want to know if you've been in love before

i want to know what bothers you

and i want to know more

i want to know your secrets and what you would rather reserve

i want to know personal things—more than i deserve

let's challenge each other

and make each other think harder

let's push each other

and make us think deeper and farther

let's talk about right and wrong

and moral roads and routes

because then, once we both leave

we'll both have something to think about

116

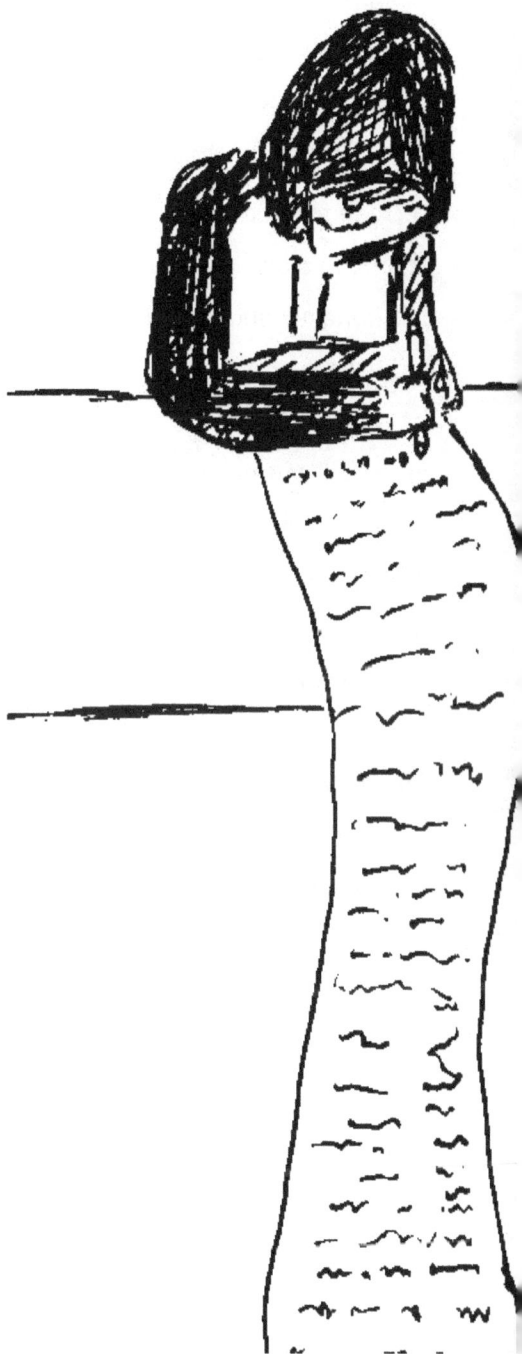

smears

complaints slip subconsciously and
>far from eloquently but always
>frequently from your lips
>putting me at my tipping point

making me long to rip open a
>paper pad

and rant about the uselessness of
>your words

endless clumps endlessly escaping
>with no substance

it boggles me how you let disgrace,
>dismay, and misplaced
>claims

blames and untamed rage

race from your thoughts to your
>voice

i hope you know you have a choice

that you are able to stop the labels

labeling this thing bad and that
>thing good

but if you just understood

you would know that once you say
>it's bad it feels worse

almost like a curse, once you

converse verses

of quote–unquote "bad" the
>situation worsens

like, for example, flies

if you complain about them, you'll realize the flies intensify

if you don't explore or account for or if you just ignore

if you don't complain or go near them

then they'll seem to disappear

all because you chose!

chose to not go close

to close mindedness, it's also called empty mindedness 'cause

when you close your mind, you stop learning

and honestly and earnestly, stopping your learning

is drastic

i'm not being ecstatic or dramatic

you need to understand this

to choose to either muse the negativity

or lose the negativity

the choice not to voice false statements

i would just like to state

that your state of mind and

the rate your mind travels

to unrelated hatred is almost impressive

depressingly impressive

but stupid and insensitive

just take initiative

and think before you speak.

(but i do fear that if you do it that way

you'll have nothing to say)

i'm sad to say that one day

you'll learn and pay

for the way you tangled words

and strangled everyone around you

118

with your angled aimed raging claims

if you always complain about today

you'll never have the good ol' days

you'll never have a bright future

to look forward to

is it because you're afraid?

afraid of the way the future will go

afraid someone will know about your past

your everlasting blast you had as of past

are you so paranoid, that you've even learned to avoid the present?

by simply talking about how things could go wrong

like a song stuck in your head, the negative has lead and consumed you

    like melted lead

you have unnecessarily and completely unfairly

subtracted the fact

that the situation

you've been placed in

is presently pleasant

a present presented and represented

by your destination and fate

and yet you face it and phrase it with dissatisfaction

and hate

it amazes me how your mind's

quickest function is rushing to nothing

chasing and racing, making sure, and being glad to point out the bad

you should try sleeping on your right side

because it sounds like you're constantly waking up on the wrong side

you'd probably tell me that

the right side isn't completely complementing or comfy

too lumpy, bumpy and slumped unevenly

clearly unclean, and you see it's seeming to be stripped of seams

making the rusted busted metal, tired wire poke me

choke me, provoke me!

oh my! poor soar me!

who's got floors to sweep

and other chores to keep

poor me, who's got a leg cramp

an amplified, leg ache or arm ache

for goodness sakes i've got an ache-ache

let me put some clarity on this rarity

poor me who's got two parents who apparently care for me

poor me for being able to sit at a table and ramble and babble and
    shovel food into my mouth

for breakfast, lunch, brunch and dinner

and of course, a coerced course of packed snacks

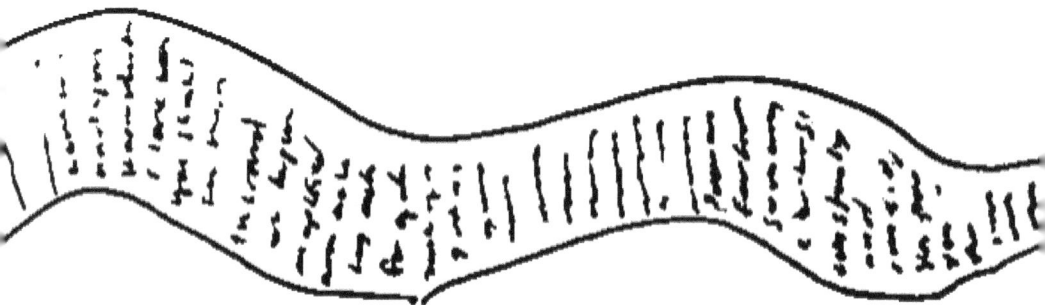

poor, poor me for being born forlorn into a

loving family

poor me for having so many siblings

constantly and consistently, trying to vastly contrast fix my mixed-up
    thoughts on complaining!

yeah, poor you, for not understanding and comprehending that

    communication is great

for language's sake!

can you not comprehend that words should not be used to fake claims

or

    complaints?

come to grips that compliments, commandments and complete

    comprehension of controversial communication is so underrated

    and often wasted

gossip and complaints

are so overrated, overstated and so utterly tasteless

you abuse and misuse the words

that could have been used and put to use

to inspire, light fires in one another

words acquire and require you to inspire others

and don't get me going on your thoughts

you ought to have fought and fight for the right thoughts

the every ever-clever thought

and brilliant chilling thoughts

your imagination is irreplaceable

you're literally able to create and make new worlds

take and shake the world

into new places, you can sink

all starting with the way that you think

so go to the sink of where you think you think

sink a mop in the warm, soapy water

then properly wash your mind

please be kind enough

to find a washcloth

then run, rub and scrub all the black, ineffective, pointless ideas, ideals,

  feels, and emotions

away from your brilliant imagination

something i hope you have

no, i know you have

you have got to try to

have to set a goal

of straightening up

and shutting up

you ask me how i can read in my mind

with ease, while reclined

as if i'm fine, as if i've got all the time

you probably think i'm deaf or blind, but

my mind is simply mindlessly minding itself

momentless miles away, swaying, swinging and singing

not listening to a thing you're pointlessly saying

i'm rudely amused with how you choose

to make everything bad news

refusing to use the power of your thoughts

for less useless ruthless and truth-less things

and that's why you lose me

my mind plays and replays memories

like screenplays while you complain

then you ask why i don't care, it's because i don't care

i don't care who said what

at school while you stuck up your nose

to who knows

and rose from your stool

i don't care that you embarrassed yourself

while trying to act cool

you'll claim that you hate rules

then complain when someone else takes them

and breaks them

you're always subconsciously coming up

and thinking up ways

to get your way

but you're going about it way wrong in the wrong way

saying, claiming falsely and complaining

does nothing to change, rearrange, erase or ease pain

nobody cares what you carelessly access and accidentally express

they only care what you're doing, how you're moving

how you're going to stop losing

and start being essentially successful

you always have a problematic proclamation

and projected problem

but you never ever savor enough energy to solve them

resolve them

or calm them

your world revolves around them

everything involves them

i'm not saying you should be happy all the time

from time to time you've got to just lie

and cry and sigh

and not even try to stop

but doing that all the time

becomes a destructive lie

note this: i've noticed

that life isn't perfect

that often it seems worthless

to try this endless, seemingly senseless

essence that powerful thoughts

can end in pain and suffering

and i must confess

that i also express

excess information

because i'm mad or sad

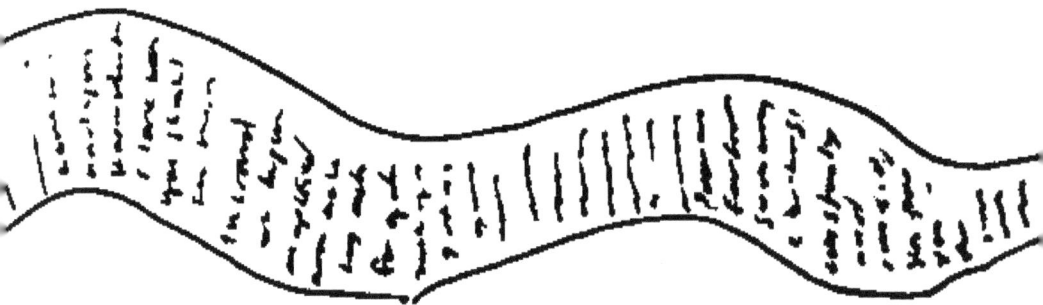

depreciative and under appreciated

and at best unsuccessful or irritated

so just know and note that this note, this poem

can be directed directly at me

nonetheless it's seriously silly how

serious and cynical

you can be

let me state

that stating the situation

is different from complaining about it

i can politely present the present circumstance

with a stance that has a solution

that's drastically different than

pointing out the potential harm without a solution

it's as bad as having a math book

and just looking at all the problems

but instead of using your head and solving them

you look at them

and expect to learn something

from your neglect

of the positivity of reality

even faintly complaining and barely snarling

as opposed to bearing and staying strong

is not only rude, but wrong

I understand the feeling of having no outlet

being upset and offset

not feeling good

always ignored and misunderstood

but you know you could

and you should

focus on the good

and you would if you understood

other's sticky, sickly situations

people who've been sit on, spit on

people who've been despised, told lies

despite their tries and cries

but somehow somewhere you find

something of despair

you nick and pick

to find things that don't please you

like a needle in a haystack

digging past the contracts, impacts and straight facts

going straight for the flaky, flip flop, non-thought opinions

then when

you find the needed needle of pointless bland

you needlessly sit cradling and complaining that you cut your hand

please, please, please

learn to be pleased

and at ease

learn to erase and face this disease

until it's at least decreased

and at best deceased

seize the moments, own it

to achieve meaning

all by leaving this idea

that words without meaning

demeaning, menacing, statements

are absolutely, abundantly wasted

tasteless and biased based

what's worse is it's on a regular basis!

learn to see and need

good thoughts and good things

please learn to be appeased

and free from pleading and pleasing only yourself

cause complaining about your situation

comes from self-pride, self lies

self-proclamation and self-protection

leaning and feeding on self esteem

'cause everything's about me

complaining is an open door to arguing

correction: pointless arguing

also labeled as worthless bickering, quarreling and fighting

people who are trained to refrain from debate

often make the common mistake of commenting

when there's no point

let me just say that debaters stick to the facts

and have endurance to have confidence in the evidence

funny, the more you learn to earn and detect respect

the more you practice practically explaining and debating complex things

to a simple mind

the more you find that sometimes

being quiet can end quarrels

silence is the best argument

halt your salty insults

opinions are the result of substantial thought

not the substitute for thought

turn your insults into instant investment in others

and interesting information, inspiring others

instead of installing insurance and reliance

on instant standards that everything has to be right

bright, light, insightful and perfect

because everything is always too much for you

too hot

too cold

too much

too bold

not worth it

just not... not perfect

too perfect

with just a little thought

and some truthful opinion

responsibility and a little wisdom

you'll learn to be bold with your tongue

and when to hold your tongue

you're either neutral at minimal or negative

never above attentive

nothing ever of importance

or deserving my attention

always defensive and sensitive

almost offensive,

but not quite that bold

endless, useless sentences

spill from your lips

filling my ears with things

that i choose not to hear

not because i fear them

and not because i can't hear them

but simply because i shouldn't be near them

you call it ignorance and negligence

i call it simple essence of genius

but you

open your eyes

there are great things in strife

please, please, please

train yourself to speak life

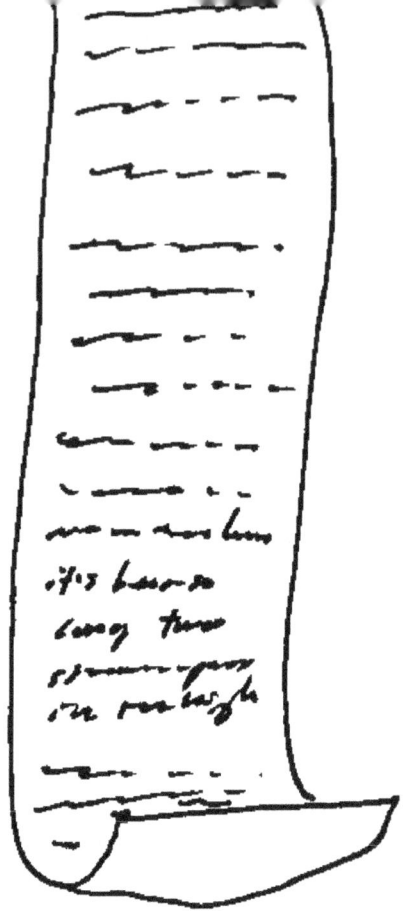

that boy

he's got his hair too short, buzzed on the top and the sides

and his shirt's too big

his pants are pulled up way too high

with a belt that doesn't match

those tan cargo pants

and of course, it's tucked in

his polo walmart shirt

clashes with his baseball cap that i hate

the one that's on a little bit too straight

and he wears it without a reason

his facial hair is uneven

his shoes are shiny

a little squeaky on the floor, a bit whiny

and you ask yourself why he

or if he knows what for

his body movements never quite match his tone

he's the kind of guy who's never on his phone

and of course, he always wears too much cologne

he's got glasses

without rims, just glasses

which are so straight they look fastened

and clasped on his face

a bit too neat, too straight for your taste

but they're symmetrical, like his briefcase

at most things he's a clumsy mess

but he's good at dumb things like sudoku and chess

if it was possible, you'd wonder if he cheats

and that makes you bite the inside of your cheeks

you look up and down and at all of him

and you cannot explain why you had to go and fall for him

three rags

three rags

sag in the wind

pinned to a board

each one of them

one of them cries

one of them curses

one of them bursts into verses

of love

one of them lives

one of them cries

one of them forgives

one of them dies

attitude (part 1)

she wakes up to a noisy alarm

"darn" she says, and sits up on her arm

she can't afford a car, so she's forced of course

to walk far in the heat

it beats down on her, as she tries not to think

at work she starts with a complaint

and moves onto something else that she hates

people ignore, people shout

and she misses the quietness of her house

she gets off work, a minute over— what a day!

she lingers for a moment, for a quick stay

she thinks about the walk home and in sinks her heart

before it's after 4 and she walks home alone

and, just her luck, it will be dark

attitude (part 2)

she wakes up to music blasting

smashing her alarm, she jumps up laughing

she showers—talking to herself too

she's too excited for coffee, she watches it brew

the sun is bright, a full glow stretched perfectly

like cursive, and the reverse of night, and a reimbursed light, a ray

she's glad she'll walk to work today

at work people throw "good mornings" over their shoulders

most people are nice, so she ignores the colder

she keeps a smile on her face

and makes sure everything's in place

she loves the walk home

the cute row of stores, and tops of other top-notch shops

we're in the same situation, me and you

dealing all day with drinks, people, and food

the only difference is attitude

sleep, please

and i am sorry

i do want to search the stars for promises with you

and i do want to see your breath because the night it cold too

and i want more than anything for my legs to ache because i'm having

    fun

but i am tired now

yes, i cannot keep my eyes open

i'm so very, very sorry i am so utterly tired

yes, let's travel the world

yes, let's answer this world's how

but please

won't you let me sleep now?

to my father

with crinkled eyes he laughs

never afraid to speak his heart

his face hides no masks

never boasting about his art

our house is love

it's packed full of memories

dad laughs with us

he has and will for centuries

he hugs his wife

with a kiss on the cheek

he blows a kiss

to a daughter in need

he works through the night

he's proudly humble

he's not afraid of the light

he picks me up when i stumble

he's watchful, like the sun over the world

he's diligent with a respectful heart

he takes care of himself, but not self-absorbed

he jokes around, but always smart

i love him so much

he's consistently glad

a strong heart but soft touch

i love him, i love you, dad

to my mother

a mom is like a clock

she knows when to walk, when to

    talk, tick-tocking

made up of some levers, some

    pushes and pulls

going unappreciated, yet everyone

    relies on her for their daily

    schedules

never dull, the schedules are full

    because of the clock we

    dismiss our struggles

'cause the clock always knows

    when to love, and the perfect

    time for snuggles

and although the clock is always moving

she makes time for choosing outfits, brewing coffee

tuning, amusing and of course soothing

she makes time for everyone, never lessening or limiting

when you talk you know she's listening

without the clock we'd all race and chase to the wrong place

we'd all embrace our inability to stop relying so much on time

but, without the clock we wouldn't know

when bedtime is

or when to take our medicine

when to wake up or to pretend— to fake to be awake

to put on our make-up

for goodness' sake, we'd be like a bat without ears

we couldn't hear so we'd never know what we're near

let's stick with one metaphor at a time here

that was a pun   .

here's another one:

clocks are handy

that didn't rhyme but it was funny

clocks make everything click

and although they may get ticked

they still make everything run without flaws

flawlessly causing perfect moments

you can't have moments without mom

unless, of course, you spelled it wrong

clocks have to be in three different places at one time

and although one thing makes them all the same

the best clock of all is the one i call mine

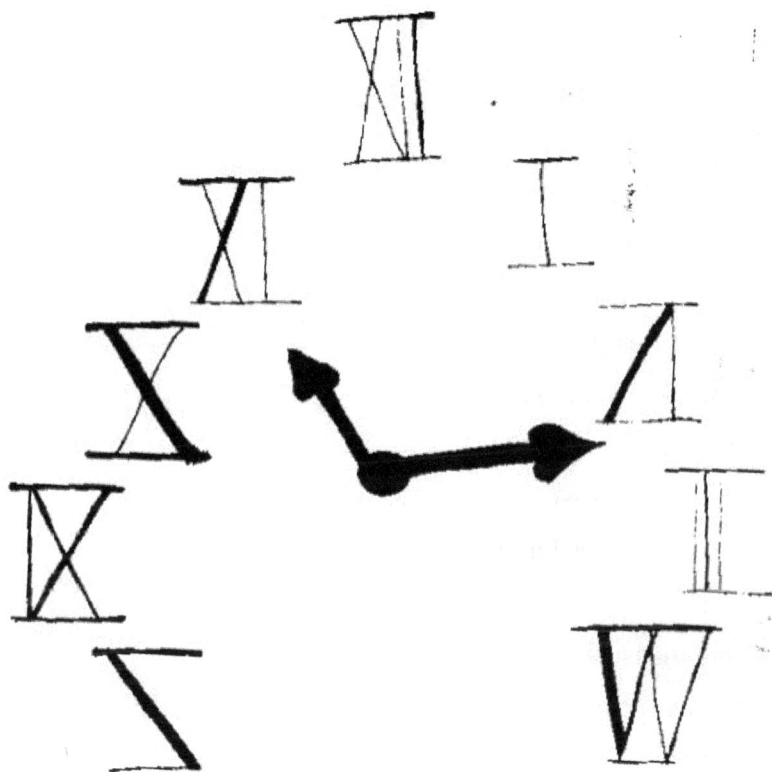

trust

our trust, it's dusty

not broken

because it hasn't been tested or invested in properly

probably because it's infested with the probability

the fear, that if tested it will shatter

like a mirror

but unlike a mirror

we can't sweep up the glass

and throw it in the trash

our tested trust will be reflected on us

trust without being tested

is like a book without a climax

like a government without tax

i insist it doesn't exist

tested trust is like instant coffee

chunky at first

but let me reassure you, my dear

it's like instant coffee

chunky at first

and then cleared

truth

there is no subjective truth

truthfully, the only true truth

comes from actual fact

but, in fact, even fact

can be taken, shaken and broken

and it always shocks me that

people who seem to talk the walk

and walk the talk

are the ones

that seem most insistent on consistently

twisting the truth

welcome to the fairy's home

there once was a fairy

of gold misty wings

firefly like battering things

you can find this fairy

of beautiful mystery

if you cross the heartache journey

start with the trail of misery

it leads to the river of jealousy

not to worry

there's a bridge filled of hope

covered in ropes

ropes that shine with faith

once you've crossed the bridge

continue to the next ridge

the seven honest hills

i must warn you, you may die

they'll swallow anyone up who lies

hike up the front of content mountain

and down the back using the trail of patience

don't forget to stop at the peace-filled fountain

remember to drink enough to be well maintained

and there just beyond the trail head

will be this golden fairy, fast asleep in her bed

i am not saying that you must be perfect

but avoiding your sin to get to where you wish to begin

is most certainly worth it

welcome to my mind

welcome to a screenplay

all about me

to be clear (or really out of fear of the truth)

this is nowhere near reality

just fiction

merely imagination.

entitled: "naked tabitha"

rated 'r' for raw, real, realistic reality

featuring insecurity

starring fear, lies and other things i've hid

introducing regret and for the first time; sin

what

i write about things i don't understand

i write about sad things, but i haven't been sad

i can't write about being happy

because i can't be sure i've experienced that either

what is poetry?

poetry is questions

collections of stupid things

and obsessions

poetry is the best of sugar coats

with seas of similes

the metaphors are boats

poetry is really a counseling session

it mainly consists of apologies and confessions

what's the difference between poems and pictures?

my sketches mean more to people than my poems

my poems mean more than they'll ever know

i suppose the supposed pictures

are supposed to look like them

pencils work with composed paper to purpose retched sketches

looking at pictures of themselves, they're flattered

cluttered with a matter of love and embarrassment

sometimes a hush

sometimes met with a blush

but as much as i enjoy drawing, not only people but drawing your
    attention

let me take a section, a second to mention a selection of differences

a picture is easy

i can admit that but it's legit that a picture only captures the outside

a poem captures what lies behind beautiful eyes

and what tries to tie lies and poker faces tightly together

a picture is temporary

a poem is forever

a picture is how you look at one time

in history, one line

a picture is one frozen emotion

a poem is what thoughts are thriving

a picture is the type of car

a poem is who's driving

in par, a picture is what you look like

a poem is who you are

when he smirks

i often imagine God with a smirk

when i wonder why he would allow sin

or how that would work

i try to explain it in graph and format

but at last he smirks and says "where's the fun in that?"

when i don't get what i want

and when i don't get straight facts

i push myself too much, too soon and too fast

but at the last second he smiles and does the task

"why didn't you help me before?" i say

he smirks, "because you didn't ask"

i'm lost, alone and hurt

i avoid prayer and my good work

i'm found, happy and strong

"oh, it's because you love me"

he smirks, "yes, love, exactly"

retreat

we sit by the campfire

for warmth and for light

we played all day

and we'll pray all night

wind

i can be perfectly comforting

or i can be perfectly devastating

deep down i wish to bring happiness

to bring wonderful aromas of scented air

i dream of having a physical existence

but, really, i don't care

it's a waste of time because i get to be everywhere

i encourage the seas

i make tea steam

i help forest fires

and vibrate telephone wires

and allow clouds to travel

to unravel, which make children marvel

although, sometimes i wonder

what would happen if i wasn't so cruel

if children kept their kites

and warmth stayed in the pool

i could make any child fly

i could take them to the moon

i think it better, though

to keep them in their room

the truth is my disguise

that i despise laughing

i appreciate their cries

i believe in destruction

i'm just who i am

i love accidents caused by my greatness

i'm courting power

yet, i submit to confusion

i'm in love with delusion and illusions

of allusions of wind

writer's block: diamante poetry

white

blank, ready

thinking, reading, writing

pen, paper, ink, thoughts

scribbling, filling, smearing

finished, mess

black

your options on death

hello, my name is death

please take a seat

let's make this quick— i'm beat

this is the fourth interview this week

name? first and last?

oh, i remember you

was it your aunt who passed?

well i was there when your distant relative died

pity, really, they could have survived

but, never mind

you look uncomfortable, uneasy maybe

come on, don't pretend you don't know who i am

you knew who i was before you were a baby

think about it, no one had to tell you who i was, friend

after all, what's the fun in living without knowing it will come to an end?

and don't play this game where you pretend to never think about me

i creep into your thoughts when you can't sleep

and then when you do, you dream of me

you worry of me when you see small children doing dangerous things

or next to dangerous, like climbing a tree

you see me in movies, in songs and in books

yes, you read of me when nobody looks

anyway, let's get to why you're here

i can lay out your options

of course, there's only four it appears

the first option you have, and the one humans can't get out of their head

is what the majority before you have chosen

live to your late eighties and then die in a hospital bed

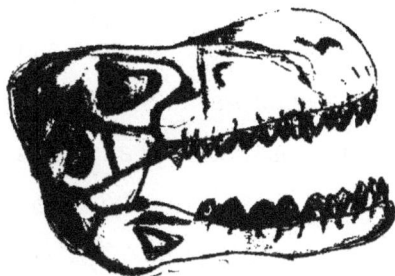

this option takes away choice

you won't know what day is your last, your last breath, last voice

the second option is suicide

lately humans seem to have caught on to this one

it's the worst way to see the other side

it's the most cowardly and selfish thing to be done

i won't sugar coat my stance on this

i don't feel bad for the ones who commit

for they did not hate themselves, they did not have self-pity

no, that all came from pride

rich, hot red pride, hovering over them—draped

where they valued their suffering above all others

they decided they were deserving of escape

your third option is to not face me at all

to walk right past me, to a greater call

there's only been one to accomplish death

straight passed me to heaven, after three days of rest

it still boggles my mind to this day

how his perfect faith slipped away

it may come as a shock to you that you can do this too

but it's true

you can move mountains with faith the size of a mustard seed

imagine what you could do with faith the size it should be

your final option is immortality—yes, living forever

existing now and whenever

all you have to do is believe that there is a new start

turn from your sinful ways, and to Him give your heart

i know it's that simple, it's easy, not hard

most men would die to live forever

they'd kill before they gave their hearts

but you have a short cut

so, choose one

i'll be in the back if you want to discuss your options further

just choose wisely

it's a miracle and a nightmare to live

but it's an adventure to die slowly

your words

your words are like water

when it's raining, i want to warm them up and add flavor

your words steam and clear my thoughts

they quench my thirst

your words are like water, pure enough to cleanse and warm enough to
    bathe in

your words are timeless like water

everybody needs them, but not everybody reads them

your words describe miracles and creation of life

your words are a necessary foundation of life

seventeen

laziness will be the death of me

my days are measured by productivity

i do productive things, but not what i'm supposed to do

like a defiant child choosing the red crayon over blue

i sit, being a lazy, self-centered, useless jerk

but unlike a child no one tells me to get to work

they only show disappointment if i don't succeed

they don't say to stop, they don't bribe, shout or plead

all because i'm a year older than sixteen

don't play the victim

the harder i work the more i earn

you can't make all the mistakes

so from others you have to learn

but life isn't hard

work hard, study hard and play your cards right

be kind, be decent, and be polite

and luck will seem to favor you

the better you better yourself

you will stop bothering yourself and be your favorite you

now is the best time to change

so take each day, each moment. savor it

save it

don't delay making it

crave success

don't worry and don't stress

and much less be true to yourself and genuine with others

life tastes like freedom if you don't cage yourself in a lie

honest souls are rare, but the demand is high

passion, math and a bike ride

passion and math

went for a bike ride

they went in the morning

they went side by side

math rode fast with logically smooth moves

his feet perfectly angled

his strides calculated, fixated and perfectly timed

passion rode swiftly

her hair zipping past the

morning mist

her hands clutched intensely

around the handlebars

her wheels traveled quickly far

math stopped to calculate

how he could double his time

but because he stopped to evaluate

passion strode right by

so, if you want to win the race

sure, you can calculate

you're strides and the mathematical methods you were taught

just always remember

that passion should not be forgot

a boy called isaiah

his eyebrows were carefree

and his eyes were intensely brown

his hoodies fit him so well it was like they was stitched into him

his hair matched the color of coffee beans so well

even someone who is not a poet would have noticed

and he would keep eye contact with me

enough that i remember his name

he looked like a little boy right out of a book

in and out

he looked like he was born to be written about

january 10th, 2018

you said you hated small talk

so instead you led and walked

the conversation to humor, imagination

and moments that burn like inspiration in my memory

you'll live for a long time in my memory

just promise that you too will remember me

you say "wanna do something?"

i say "i'm in"

it might be that you have a lisp

or maybe it's that your laugh is so genuine

we hadn't seen each other in four years

but i didn't search for cares, nor fears

but more reasons to remember you

soon at everything we laughed, yes, we laughed at all

it was as if no time had passed at all

glasses

glasses are beautiful things

they fit personalities

they complement outfits

they can be big and quirky

or small, lurking in the corners and focusing on the details

oh, and sunglasses are cool

perfect for driving and hiking trails

matching part of your outfit

to match shoes or maybe painted nails

they can be for the look, a little art

they can help you look smart

they give you a little peak

into people's personalities

glasses are wonderful things

they can be anything you want them to be

oh—and they also help me see

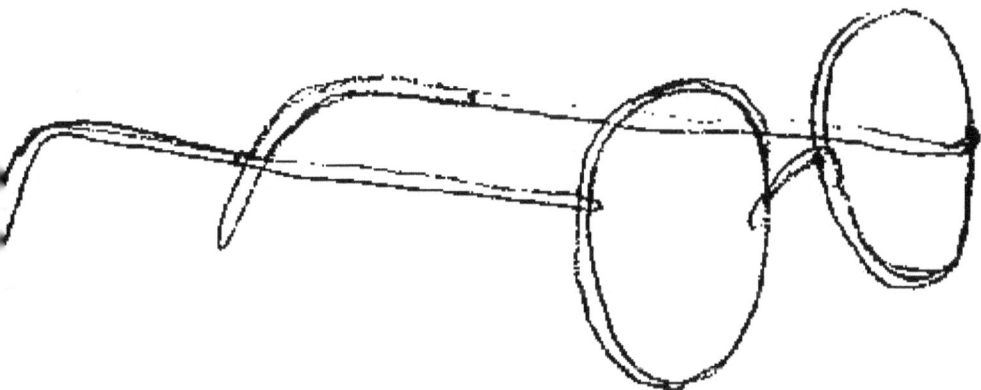

one more poem

i don't know what to write about

which i must confess is a first

i hope this inspires and sounds okay

despite not having a sounded verse

i don't know what to write about

but that's okay 'cause i can write

i'm not quite sure where this poem will go

but that's okay, it will work out, it's alright

i don't know how long this will be

i will write until i run out of words

or until they stop coming to me

my hope is that they won't stop

this has started to form into something okay

maybe good enough to read aloud

or good enough to read to myself one day

or read in front of a crowd

this has started to turn into a poem i may keep

which is good, 'cause my poem count is low for a poet

maybe one day i'll decide to delete it

but here's one more they'll read when i'm gone

this has turned into a so-so poem

that will catch every other eye

some will read it and be in awe

others will think to themselves "why?"

and if it helps, i don't really know what i just wrote

but here it is

one more poem

one lacking storyline and depth

but at least i can say i put in my two cents before my death

climbing trees

i hope this home never changes

the mismatched coffee mugs

and hugs from little children

and nudges from older, smug brothers

and little kids with smudges of candy and dirt

around their little smirks

and their dirty shirts

proving they were outside living fully

i hope the walls stay painted dully

and the chairs stay on the right sides of the table

i hope i'll visit just as often as i'm able

and once more

i hope the trees stay strong

so we can climb them until our arms are sore

and we can soar through the wind on the ropes we tied there

and i hope the dirt stays soft so we can

walk without shoes, our feet bare

i hope the relay races we make up stay so i can win

and i hope the dam builds up in the creak so we can swim

i hope the zipline stays as unsafe as the trampoline

and i hope the clouds don't mind that we love the lightning

i hope the shoe closet stays as full as our conversations

and that the toy boxes that were for us are used by the grandkids

i hope the driveway stays steep

because of the rain and the bike skids

i hope our favorite books remain coffee stained and torn

i hope the hand—me—downs are happily worn

these bookshelves better stay organized

and the ceiling broken

i hope the carpet stays the color of paint and sparkly hot glue

and the real talk in the tree house better stay as long as the sky is blue

this home should stay the best place to stay up till 3 in the morning

talking about things that would otherwise be boring

this house should be the place where you can find my father snoring

this is the best place to swim and the best place to run

we have the best view of the moon, the city, the stars and the sun

the best place a guest could be welcomed and for the Lord to be
   praised

the best place for home-church and the best place for kittens to be
   raised

wherever i go i'll tell this to people who have never been here before

i promise i will visit as often as i am able

and once more

www.ingramcontent.com/pod-product-compliance
Lightning Source LLC
LaVergne TN
LVHW041220080426
835508LV00011B/1021

9 7 8 1 9 3 6 1 4 7 1 7 5